1,000,000 Books

are available to read at

Forgotten Books

www.ForgottenBooks.com

Read online
Download PDF
Purchase in print

ISBN 978-1-332-42528-0
PIBN 10425314

This book is a reproduction of an important historical work. Forgotten Books uses state-of-the-art technology to digitally reconstruct the work, preserving the original format whilst repairing imperfections present in the aged copy. In rare cases, an imperfection in the original, such as a blemish or missing page, may be replicated in our edition. We do, however, repair the vast majority of imperfections successfully; any imperfections that remain are intentionally left to preserve the state of such historical works.

Forgotten Books is a registered trademark of FB &c Ltd.
Copyright © 2018 FB &c Ltd.
FB &c Ltd, Dalton House, 60 Windsor Avenue, London, SW19 2RR.
Company number 08720141. Registered in England and Wales.

For support please visit www.forgottenbooks.com

1 MONTH OF FREE READING

at
www.ForgottenBooks.com

By purchasing this book you are eligible for one month membership to ForgottenBooks.com, giving you unlimited access to our entire collection of over 1,000,000 titles via our web site and mobile apps.

To claim your free month visit:
www.forgottenbooks.com/free425314

* Offer is valid for 45 days from date of purchase. Terms and conditions apply.

English
Français
Deutsche
Italiano
Español
Português

www.forgottenbooks.com

Mythology Photography **Fiction**
Fishing Christianity **Art** Cooking
Essays Buddhism Freemasonry
Medicine **Biology** Music **Ancient Egypt** Evolution Carpentry Physics
Dance Geology **Mathematics** Fitness
Shakespeare **Folklore** Yoga Marketing
Confidence Immortality Biographies
Poetry **Psychology** Witchcraft
Electronics Chemistry History **Law**
Accounting **Philosophy** Anthropology
Alchemy Drama Quantum Mechanics
Atheism Sexual Health **Ancient History**
Entrepreneurship Languages Sport
Paleontology Needlework Islam
Metaphysics Investment Archaeology
Parenting Statistics Criminology
Motivational

EDWARD HERON-ALLEN

Some Side-lights upon Edward FitzGerald's Poem

"THE RUBA'IYAT OF OMAR KHAYYĀM"

Being the Substance of a Lecture delivered at the
Grosvenor Crescent Club and Women's Institute
on the 22nd March 1898

LONDON
H. S. NICHOLS Ltd.
39 CHARING CROSS ROAD W.C.
1898

Printed and Published by
H S. NICHOLS, LTD ,
39 CHARING CROSS ROAD, W.C

TO

Professor E. B. COWELL, M.A.,

Professor of Sanskrit in the University of Cambridge.

Dear Professor Cowell,

It was to you that Edward FitzGerald owed his knowledge of the Persian language, and his introduction to the Ruba'iyat of Omar Khayyám. It is to you that I owe, not only my grateful thanks for much sympathy and assistance in my own work as a humbler student of those quatrains, but also the clue which started me upon the researches whose results are embodied in this opusculum. As a slight acknowledgment of these favours I have ventured to address my observations to you,

And I am, with great respect,

Very sincerely yours,

EDWARD HERON-ALLEN.

London, 22nd March, 1898.

SOME SIDE-LIGHTS UPON EDWARD FITZGERALD'S POEM, "THE RUBA'IYAT OF OMAR KHAYYĀM."

THERE is material for much subtle argument—material indeed for discussion such as is dear to the souls of the self-proclaimed Wise Men of the East—in the following problem: Did Omar Khayyām give fame to Edward FitzGerald, or did Edward FitzGerald give European fame to Omar Khayyām? And by fame I mean, not the respect paid to a great poet by students of the language in which he wrote, but that far-reaching and universal popularity which enshrouds the names of Edward FitzGerald and Omar Khayyām in every quarter of the known world where the English language is spoken by natives or colonists. Though the recent utterances of Colonel Hay, the United States Ambassador to this country, may seem, even to Omar's most fervent devotees, a trifle exaggerated,[1] it is not, I think, too much to say that, even in this latter half of the 19th century, when the cult of particular poets has drawn bands of men and women together and given us Shakespeare Societies, Shelley Societies, Browning Societies, and the like, there is no freemasonry so infallible, no sympathy

---

1. *Daily Chronicle*, 9th December, 1897.—"The exquisite beauty, the faultless form, the singular grace of those amazing stanzas, were not more wonderful than the depth and breadth of their profound philosophy, their knowledge of life, their dauntless courage, their serene facing of the ultimate problems of life and death. . . . I came upon a literal translation of the Ruba'iyat, and I saw that not the least remarkable quality of FitzGerald's poem was its fidelity to the original. . . . It is not to the disadvantage of the later poet that he followed so closely in the footsteps of the earlier. . . . There is not a hill-post in India or a village in England where there is not a coterie to whom Omar Khayyām is a familiar friend and a bond of union."

so profound, as that which unites the lovers of the quatrains of Omar Khayyām, in the form in which they have been made known to us by the beautiful, the eternal poem of " Old Fitz " —the Laird of Littlegrange.

The incunabulum, the earliest archive of the cult, is admittedly the single verse attributed to the ghost of Omar (by whom it was recited in a dream to his mother) and recorded in the " History of the Religion of the Ancient Persians, Parthians and Medes," by Dr. Thomas Hyde, Regius Professor of Arabic in the University of Oxford, in the year 1700.[2] This is the quatrain which was rendered by FitzGerald in the Introduction to his poem:

> O thou who burn'st in Heart for those who burn
> In Hell, whose fires thyself should feed in turn;
> How long be crying, " Mercy on them, God!"
> Why, who art thou to teach, and He to learn.[3]

The German renderings of Josef von Hammer-Purgstall[4] and Friedrich Rückert[5] would not by themselves have called Omar to the position which he holds to-day among the poets of the world, and without the poem of FitzGerald the record of the astronomer-poet might have closed with the publication of his treatise upon Algebra and the higher mathematics, which was given to the world in 1851 by Dr. Woepcke, Professor of Mathe-

---

[2]. "Veterum Persarum et Parthorum et Medorum religionis historia." Oxford, 1700; 2nd Edition, 1760. Appendix, pp. 529, 530.

[3]. Dr. Hyde's rendering runs:

> O combustus combustus Combustione!
> Vae, a te est Ignis Gehennae Accensis!
> Quousque dicis, *Omaro misericors esto?*
> Quousque Deum, *Caput Misericordiae*, docebis?

which is a more correct rendering than FitzGerald's of the original, which is C. 1, L. 769, B. 755, S. P. 453, B. II. 537, W. 488, N 459. Persian

اي سوختهٔ سوختهٔ سوختني   ولي كه آتش دوزخ از تو افروختني
تاكه گوئي كه بر عمر رحمت كن   حق را تو كجائي رحمت اموختني

[4]. "Geschichte der schönen Redekünste Persiens, &c." Vienna, 1818, p. 80, 20.

[5]. "Grammatik, Poetik und Rhetorik der Perser," herausgegeben von W. Pertsch. Gotha, 1874.

matics in the University of Bonn ^/r.[6] Dr. Woepcke has pointed out in the Introduction to his translation that the Algebra of Omar Khayyām first attracted the notice of mathematicians in 1742, when a Dutch *savant*, Gerard Meerman, called attention to a manuscript of his treatise, bequeathed by one Warner to the town of Leyden. The citation occurs in the Introduction to Meerman's " Specimen calculi fluxionalis." Succeeding mathematicians called attention to the work; but the first important consideration that it received was at the hands of L. A. Sedillot, who announced in the *Nouveau Journal Asiatique*, in May, 1834, the discovery of an incomplete MS. of the same treatise in the Bibliothèque Royale in Paris. It was reserved for Professor Libri to discover, in the same place, a complete MS. of the work, and it was from the Leyden MS., the Sedillot fragment, and the Libri MS. that Dr. Woepcke edited his admirable text and translation. In his Introduction Dr. Woepcke gives a translation of the account of Omar from the Tarīkh ūl hukamā of Jamal ud Din 'Ali, which has been so often quoted in articles upon the poet,[7] and observes upon it that Omar " is a detestable man, but an unequalled astronomer; he is perhaps a heretic, but surely he is a philosopher of the first order." This opinion would appear to have been shared by Elphinstone,[8] who, in his account of Cabul, places on record what may, perhaps, be looked upon as an undesirable precursor of the Omar Khayyām Club. He says: "Another sect, which is sometimes confounded with the Sufis, is one which bears the name of Moollah Zukkee, who was its great patron in Cabul. Its followers hold that all the prophets were impostors and all revelation an invention. They seem very doubtful of the truth of a future state, and even of the being of

6. " L'Algèbre d'Omar Alkhâyyami," publiee, traduite et accompagnée d'extraits de manuscrits inédits par F. Woepcke. Paris, 1851.

7. *Vide* Nathan H. Dole's Multivariorum edition of the " Ruba'iyat of Omar Khayyâm." Boston (Mass.), 1896. Vol. ii., pp. 457-461.

8. The Hon. Mountstuart Elphinstone. "An account of the Kingdom of Caubul and its Dependencies in Persia, Tartary, and India." London, 1815. Ch. v, p. 209.

a God. Their tenets appear to be very ancient, and are precisely those of the old Persian poet Khayyām (*sic*, Kheioom), whose works exhibit such specimens of impiety as probably never were equalled in any other language. Khayyām dwells particularly on the existence of evil, and taxes the Supreme Being with the introduction of it in terms which can scarcely be believed. The Sufis have unaccountably pressed this writer into their service; they explain away some of his blasphemies by forced interpretations; others they represent as innocent freedoms and reproaches such as a lover may pour out against his beloved. The followers of Moollah Zukkee are said to take the full advantage of their release from the fear of hell and the awe of a Supreme Being, and to be the most dissolute and unprincipled profligates in the kingdom. Their opinions nevertheless are cherished in secret, and are said to be very prevalent among the licentious nobles of the Court of Shah Mahmoud." And, notwithstanding that Professor Cowell made the Algebra of Omar Khayyām the text for his article in the *Calcutta Review* (January, 1858), here, but for FitzGerald, might have rested the fame of him who, as Dr. Hyde described him, was "one of the Eight who settled the Jalāli era, in 1079," a computation of time which, says Gibbon,[9] surpassed the Julian and approached the accuracy of the Gregorian style.

The object of the present essay, however, is, not to analyse the quatrains composed by, or attributed to Omar Khayyām, but to examine by the light of diligent research the poem of Edward FitzGerald, which was founded upon and took its title from those quatrains, or رباعیات (ruba'iyat). Almost from the day upon which FitzGerald's poem first saw the light, a controversy, in which question and doubt have been uppermost, has raged round the problem of how far it can claim to be regarded as a correct rendering—I will

---

9. "Decline and Fall of the Roman Empire," chap. lvii., Gibbing's edition, 1890, vol. iv., p. 180. *Vide* also Dr. Hyde, *loc. cit.*, chap. xvi., pp. 200-211.

not say translation, for that is an expression that cannot be properly applied to it—of the original quatrains. I have remarked in another place,[10] "A translation pure and simple it is *not*, but a translation in the most classic sense of the term it undoubtedly is." Since expressing that view, however, I have had occasion to modify it. Prof. Charles Eliot Norton has summed up the position in a passage unsurpassed in the literature of criticism.[11] He says: "FitzGerald is to be called 'translator' only in default of a better word, one which should express the poetic transfusion of a poetic spirit from one language to another, and the re-representation of the ideas and images of the original in a form not altogether diverse from their own, but perfectly adapted to the new conditions of time, place, custom and habit of mind in which they reappear. . . . It is the work of a poet inspired by the work of a poet; not a copy, but a reproduction; not a translation, but the re-delivery of a poetic inspiration."

FitzGerald's poem is, however, something more than this. Stated in the fewest possible words, the poem familiar to English readers as the "Ruba'iyat of Omar Khayyām" is the expressed result of FitzGerald's entire course of Persian studies. There are many isolated lines and ideas, and more than one entire quatrain for which diligent study has revealed no corresponding passages in the original quatrains of Omar Khayyām—notably, for instance, the quatrain:

    O Thou who Man of baser Earth did'st make,
    And ev'n with Paradise devised the Snake:
    For all the Sin wherewith the Face of Man
    Is blacken'd—Man's forgiveness give—and take!

and the opening quatrain, which Mr. Aldis Wright, the editor of his "Letters and Literary Remains,"[12] says "is entirely his own." Even Professor Cowell has said, *ex cathedrâ*, "there is no original for the line about the snake," and attri-

---

10. "The Ruba'iyat of Omar Khayyām," translated by Edward Heron-Allen. London, 1898.
11. In the *North American Review*, October, 1869.
12. London, 1889. Macmillan, 3 vols.

butes the last line to a mistake of FitzGerald's in translating a quatrain from Nicolas, which led him to "invent" the line. We shall presently see that this is not so, save in so far as that FitzGerald took these lines by a process of <u>automatic cerebration</u>, not from Omar, but from other sources. The manner in which he wrote his poem must be borne in mind. Professor Cowell, writing to me (under date 8th July, 1897), says: "I am quite sure that he did not make a literal prose version first; he was too fond of getting the strong vivid impression of the original as a whole. He pondered this over and over afterwards, and altered it in his lonely walks, sometimes approximating nearer to the original, and often diverging farther. He was always aiming at some strong and worthy equivalent; verbal accuracy he disregarded." Composing his poem in this manner, with the original ruba'iyat not before him, all the impressions stored in his brain as the result of his extensive studies of Persian poetry, and Persian history, manners and customs, were present in his mind, and the echoes of those studies are clearly recognisable in the lines and passages which have defied the research of students of the original quatrains.

That no one should have called attention to this before, surprises me, for the process was indicated clearly by Professor Cowell in his note upon the opening lines of quatrain No. 33:

> Earth could not answer; nor the seas that mourn
> In flowing Purple, of their Lord forlorn.

FitzGerald corresponded with Professor Cowell upon these two very lines—or rather upon the idea contained in them—in March, 1857, but it was reserved for the latter to call attention to the fact that they were taken from the Mantik-ut-Tair (the Parliament, or Language of Birds) of Ferīd-ud-dīn Attār. FitzGerald himself never acknowledged in his printed works the assistance of anyone, or (except in the case of Mr. Binning's Journal) the sources of any of his information, but I have followed the clue given by Professor Cowell, and by dint of reading every work to which FitzGerald refers in his letters, during the time when he was composing his poem, I have traced the actual originals of those debatable lines, and discovered the sources from which his information concerning Persia and the Persians was derived.

FitzGerald, in 1845, was repelled rather than attracted by Oriental study, as we know from the contempt he expressed concerning Eliot Warburton's "The Crescent and the Cross," published in that year; but in 1846 Professor Cowell was translating some Odes of Hāfiz,[13] and sent some of his renderings to FitzGerald, who was greatly impressed by them. It was not, however, until 1853 that, fired by Cowell's enthusiasm, he addressed himself seriously to the study of the Persian language, reading as a foundation Sir Wm. Jones's Persian Grammar, which exactly suited him, as all the examples of the values are given in beautiful lines from Hāfiz, Sa'adi, and other Persian poets. He records buying a Gulistān (of Sa'adi)[14] whilst still studying the Grammar, but it did not very greatly influence his later work. In 1854 he read and paraphrased Jāmī's "Salāmān and Absāl," which he printed for private circulation in 1856, and reprinted in 1871. After this came Hāfiz (in 1857), but by this time he had received from Professor Cowell a copy of the MS. of Omar Khayyām, which Cowell had found uncatalogued and unknown among the Ouseley MSS. in the Bodleian Library at Oxford. It was about this time also that he began to correspond with the eminent French Orientalist Garçin de Tassy, about the latter's critical essay upon the Mantik-ut-Tair of Ferīd-ud-dīn Attār, with which he had already become acquainted in De Sacy's notes to the Pend Namah of the same poet;[15] and early in 1857 he borrowed

13. These were not published until September, 1854, when they appeared anonymously in *Fraser's Magazine*, and called forth further praise from FitzGerald.
14. E. B. Eastwick. "The Gulistān, or Rose Garden." London, 1852.
15. "Pend-Nameh, ou Livre des Conseils de Férid eddin Attar." Traduit et publié par M. le Bon Silvestre de Sacy. Paris, 1819. At p. 41 of this work the parable of Jesus and the bitter water in the jar is given at length in French

a MS. of the original poem from Napoleon Newton, one of the dons of Hertford College, Oxford. The two poems, the Ruba'iyat and the Mantik-ut-Tair, took violent hold of his imagination, and already, in March, 1857, he had completed "twenty pages of a metrical sketch of the Mantik." This sketch, though eventually finished, was never published until after his death, when it was included in his "Letters and Literary Remains"; but the influence of the original upon his Ruba'iyat of Omar Khayyām

and Persian, and at pp. 168-173 there is a complete *résumé* of the entire Mantik-ut-Tair. Though we know that this volume formed part of FitzGerald's course of study, I have not made it one of the works to be analysed in this essay, for the reason that its teaching was, without doubt, merged in that of the same author's Mantik-ut-Tair. At the same time, besides the passage cited in Note 38, there are several passages to which one might refer in such an essay as this, *exempli gratia*, the story from Sa'adi's Mujaliss, which is worthy of transcription in its entirety: "One day, Ibrahim bin Adhem was seated at the gate of his palace, and his pages stood near him in a line. A dervish, bearing the insigna of his condition, came up and attempted to enter the palace. 'Old man,' said the pages, 'whither goest thou?' 'I am going into this caravanserai,' said the old man. The pages answered, 'It is not a caravanserai; it is the palace of Ibrahim, Shah of Balkh.' Ibrahim caused the old man to be brought before him, and said to him: 'Darvish, this is my palace.' 'To whom,' asked the old man, 'did this palace originally belong?' 'To my grandfather.' 'After him, who was its owner?' 'My father.' 'And to whom did it pass on his death?' 'To me.' 'When you die, to whom will it belong?' 'To my son.' 'Ibrahim,' said the Darvish, 'a place whither one enters and whence another departs is not a palace, it is a caravanserai.'" We have here a powerful suggestion of FitzGerald's 17th and 45th quatrains:

> Think, in this batter'd Caravanserai,
> Whose Portals are alternate Night and Day,
> How Sultān after Sultān with his Pomp
> Abode his destined Hour, and went his way.

> 'Tis but a Tent where takes his one day's rest
> A Sultān to the realm of Death address
> The Sultān rises, and the dark Ferrāsh
> Strikes, and prepares it for another Guest.

At pp. 236-244, we have a collection of passages in eulogy of generosity, and at p. 309, de Sacy quotes an ode of Shahi containing the image of the rose tearing asunder its garment of purple silk,

تا گل ازباد صبح بوی تو یافت   جامها پاره کرد بر تن خویش

which suggests FitzGerald's No. 14:

> Look to the blowing Rose about us, "Lo,
> Laughing," she says, "into the world I blow,
> At once the silken tassel of my Purse
> Tear, and its Treasure on the Garden throw."

Such parallels might be greatly extended, but, for the most part, the images are repeated in the Mantik-ut-Tair.

was so great, that whole quatrains and a great many isolated lines came, consciously or unconsciously, from the Mantik into his poem. It is not in any way surprising that this was so, for Attār's poems are a perfect reflection of the Ruba'iyat of Omar, on which it is more than probable that much of their philosophy was founded, seeing that Ferīd-ud-dīn Attār was born at Nishapur in Khorasān four years before Omar Khayyām died there, and was, no doubt, brought up to revere the recently deceased poet-mathematician and his works. In 1857 FitzGerald received from De Tassy his magnificent text of the Mantik; but De Tassy's translation was not published until 1863, so FitzGerald had nothing but the introductory analysis to help him, Professor Cowell being at that time in India. By June, 1857, he had received from Professor Cowell a copy of the MS. of Omar Khayyām in the Bengal Asiatic Society's Library at Calcutta,[16] and addressed himself at once to the arduous task of deciphering it. We may infer with some degree of certainty that his poem was principally constructed on the foundation of the Bodleian MS. from the fact that within three weeks of the arrival of the Calcutta MS. he had practically finished the first draft of his poem, having surveyed the Calcutta MS. "rather hastily," as he himself says. During the remaining months of 1857 he polished and prepared his poem for the press, and sent it (in January, 1858) to *Fraser's Magazine* for publication; but the editor of that eminently respectable serial did not consider it, evidently, up to the standard demanded by his other contributors and readers, and in January, 1859, FitzGerald took it away from him, added a few of the more antinomian quatrains that he had suppressed out of consideration for Fraser's families, schools, and the Young Person, and gave them to our mutual friend "little Quaritch" to sell   The oft-told tale of how the edition fell

16. This MS. has been lost or stolen, so that Professor Cowell's copy is now the only means of ascertaining what were the materials from which FitzGerald worked. A copy is now being remade from Professor Cowell's copy for the Asiatic Society's Library in Calcutta.

from grace to "the penny box," and rose thence to seven guineas a copy, has become a gem of classic antiquity, like most of the anecdotes concerning Omar, FitzGerald and FitzGerald's poem. This particular story, however, has paled into insignificance, for a copy of this first edition was sold at auction on the 10th February, 1898, to Mr. Quaritch for £21, and I have received an offer from America of £45 for a copy. Meanwhile, he had read Mr. Binning's charming journal of his travels in Persia,[17] and culled therefrom the historical, topographical, legendary and sociological information that is to be found in the notes to his Ruba'iyat, including a prose translation of the quatrain which appeared in his second edition, and which he quotes in his notes to the third and fourth editions:

> The Palace that to Heav'n his pillars threw,
> And Kings the forehead on his threshold drew—
> I saw the solitary Ringdove there,
> And "Coo, coo, coo," she cried; and "Coo, coo, coo."[18]

(C. 419, L. 627, B. 619, S. P. 347, P. 140, B. ii. 459, W. 392, N. 350.) This is merely quoted by Mr. Binning, without reference to Omar Khayyām, but FitzGerald identified it, of course, in the Calcutta MS. where it occurs, though it is not to be found in the Bodleian MS.[19]

In 1867, Mons. Nicolas published his text and prose translation,[20] which, as FitzGerald tells us, "reminded him of

---

[17]. Robert B. M. Binning. "A Journal of Two Years' Travel in Persia, Ceylon, &c." London, 1857. Vol. ii., p. 20.

[18] ان قصر که با چرخ همی زد پهلو   بر درگه او شهان نهادندی رو
    دیدیم که بر کنگره‌اش فاخته‌ای   آواز همیداد که کو کو کو کو

[19]. FitzGerald had also before him a very similar passage from the Pend Nameh of Attār (*vide* Note 15), to which de Sacy had appended notes from Omar Khayyām and other poets, which impressed it on his mind. The passage runs as follows: "Though thou may'st rear thy palace towards heaven, thou wilt one day be buried beneath the earth. Though thy power and strength equal those of Rustam, thou shalt be one day reduced like Bahrām to the abode of the tomb."

گر عمارت را بری بر آسمان   عاقبت زیر زمین گردی نهان
گر چو رستم موکب و زورت بود   جای چون بهرام در گورت بود

[20]. J. B. Nicolas. "Les Quatrains de Kheyam traduits du Persan." Paris, 1867.

several things and instructed him in others," and his interest being once more aroused in Omar Khayyām, he prepared his second edition (that of 1868), in which we find several new quatrains (ten in all), the originals of most of which are common to Nicolas's translation and the Calcutta MS. FitzGerald's note upon the dying utterance of Nizām ul Mulk came from De Tassy's translation of the Mantik-ut-Tair, which he sent to FitzGerald in exchange for a copy of this translation by Nicolas. After this, FitzGerald practically dropped the study of Persian literature; he reduced the number of his quatrains to 101, and gave us what for all practical purposes was the final form of his poem in the third edition (of 1872).

In this recapitulation of FitzGerald's study of the Ruba'iyat, I fear that I have perforce travelled over well-worn ground, but it has been necessary for the purpose I have in view of showing how those studies influenced his poem. We have, then, as his acknowledged materials:

(i.) The Odes of Hāfiz, translated by Professor Cowell in 1846, and published in 1854.
(ii.) Sir William Jones's Grammar of the Persian Language.
(iii.) The Gulistān of Sa'adi.
(iv.) The Salāmān and Absāl of Jāmī.
(v.) The Mantik-ut-Tair of Attār.
(vi.) Binning's Journal.
And of Omar Khayyām's Ruba'iyat,
(vii.) The Bodleian MS.
(viii.) The Calcutta MS.
(ix.) Nicolas's Translation and Text.

I propose to examine these materials in their chronological order, and call attention to those passages whose echoes we find in FitzGerald's poem.

I. It is not surprising that the future "translator" (in default of that better word for which Professor Norton appeals) of the Ruba'iyat of Omar Khayyām should first have been attracted to the study of Persian by the Odes of Hāfiz as presented by Professor Cowell's translations, and the examples of Sir Wm. Jones, for the two poets are brothers in song indeed. There is recorded a saying of the great Akbar himself that "an ode of Hāfiz is the wine, and a quatrain of Omar is the relish."[21] I take the following parallels from the Odes of Hāfiz translated by Cowell:

Cowell's Hafiz.	FitzGerald's Ruba'iyat.
I. Thou knowest not the secrets of futurity, There are hidden games behind the Veil; do not despair.	52. A moment guess'd—then back behind the Fold Immerst of Darkness round the Drama roll'd Which, for the Pastime of Eternity, He doth himself contrive, enact, behold.

There is a parallel for this in the Bodleian MS. :

    94. To speak plain language and not in parables,
        we are the pieces and heaven plays the game,
        we are played together in a baby game upon the chessboard
            of existence,
        and one by one return to the box of non-existence.[22]

FitzGerald took from this his quatrain :

    69. But helpless Pieces of the Game He plays
        Upon this Chequer-board of Nights and Days
        Hither and thither moves, and checks, and slays,
        And one by one, back in the Closet lays.

So that the sentiment of No. 52 comes clearly from Hāfiz.

II. Rest not thy trust on that night-patrolling star,[23] for that cunning thief Hath stolen Kawus' crown and the girdle of Kay Khusraw.	9-10. And this first Summer Month[24] that brings the Rose Shall take Jamshyd and Kaikobād away. Well, let it take them! What have we to do With Kaikobād the Great, or Kaikhosru ?

    21. H. S. Jarrett. Ain-i-Akbari, by Abu Fazl-i-Allami. Calcutta, 1891. Pt. ii., p. 392.

[22] از روی حقیقتی نه از روی مجاز   ما لعبتكانیم و فلك لعبت باز
بلزیچه همی كنیم بر نطع وجود   رفتیم بصندوق عدم یك یك باز

    23. *i.e.*, The Moon.
    24. Moon—Month = Mah (مه‍ ‌ماه) Persian synonym.

V. The morning dawns and the cloud has woven a canopy, The morning draught, my friends, the morning draught! . . . It is strange that at such a season They shut up the wine-tavern! oh, hasten! Have they still shut up the door of the tavern? Open, oh thou Keeper of the Gates!	3. And, as the Cock crew, those who stood before The Tavern shouted, "Open then the Door! You know how little while we have to stay, And, once departed, may return no more."

The parallel here is obvious, the more so as there is no quatrain in the Bodleian or Calcutta MSS. that conveys this picture of the unopened tavern.

VII. The foundations of our penitence, whose solidity seemed as of stone— See, a cup of glass, how easily hath it shattered them	93-4. Indeed, the Idols I have loved so long . . . . . . Have drown'd my Glory in a shallow Cup . . . . . . Indeed, indeed Repentance oft before I swore . . . And then and then came Spring, and Rose-in-hand My thread - bare Penitence a-pieces tore.
Since from this caravanserai with its two gates departure is inevitable.	17. Think, in this battered Caravanserai Whose Portals are alternate Night and Day, How Sultàn after Sultàn with his Pomp Abode his destined Hour, and went his way.
	45. 'Tis but a Tent where takes his one day's rest A Sultàn to the realm of Death address; &c. &c. (C. 95 & 110.)

It will be borne in mind that FitzGerald read these Odes over again in *Fraser's Magazine* (as he himself indicates in his "Letters") whilst his poem was in course of construction. It is also worthy of remark that he took his *incorrect* transliteration of Jalal-ud-dīn Rūmī—"Jellaledin," to which more than one writer has referred, from this article.

II. We have not, however, finished with Hāfiz. His lines predominate in Sir Wm. Jones's Grammar, and these isolated passages, with some from other poets, evidently fixed themselves in FitzGerald's mind when he was deciphering them word by word for the purpose of learning the language.

Jones's Quotations.[26]	FitzGerald's Ruba'iyat.
p. 22. Boy, bring the wine, for the season of the rose approaches; let us again break our vows of repentance in the midst of the roses.[26]	94. Quoted above.

The phrase *fasl-i-gul* (فصل گل), "the season of roses," is a common Persian expression to indicate spring, but I have not found it connected with the breaking of vows of penitence in FitzGerald's MSS. of Omar Khayyām. It may be observed that this passage was his first introduction to the connection of the Rose and Nightingale, so constantly recurring in Persian *belles-lettres*.[27]

p. 27. The Cypress is graceful, but thy shape is more graceful than the cypress.[28]	41. The Cypress-slender minister of wine.
p. 89. It is morning; boy, fill the cup with wine, the rolling heaven makes no delay; therefore hasten. The sun of the wine rises from the east of the cup: if thou seekest the delights of mirth, leave thy sleep.[29]	

25. The Seventh Edition. London, 1809.

[26] ساقي بيار باده که آمد زمان گل   تا بشکنيم توبه دکر در ميان گل

27. Save in No. 6 and remotely in No. 96, FitzGerald has not introduced the loves of the Nightingale and the Rose into his poem. There are many references to it in Jones. *Cf.* pp. 80, 90, 112, 120, etc.

[28] ماه نيکوست ولي روي تو زيباتر ازوست سرو دلجوست ولي قد تو دلجوتر ازوست

[29] صبحست ساقيا قدحي پر بمراب کن   دور فلك درنك ندارد متاب کن
خورشيد مي زمشرق ساغر طلوع کرد   گر برگ عيش ميطلبي ترك خواب کن

Here we have again the inspiration for the opening quatrains cited above.

p. 102. By the approach of Spring and the return of December the leaves of our life are continually folded.[30]

8. The leaves of life keep falling one by one.

This is a distich culled by Sir Wm. Jones from Omar Khayyám himself, and from a quatrain which occurs in the Calcutta MS. (No. 500), but FitzGerald was evidently "reminded of it" by Nicolas's text, where it is No. 402, for the line does not occur in his first edition. It was doubtless the above quotation that originally fixed it in his mind.

On p. 106. The spider holds the veil in the palace of Caesar;
The owl stands sentinel on the watch-tower of Afrasiab.[31]

This is a constantly recurring illustration of the vanity of earthly glory in Persian *belles-lettres*. FitzGerald probably took the first half of his quatrain No. 16 from this:

They say the Lion and the Lizard keep
The courts where Jamshyd gloried and drank deep.

The second half comes from the Calcutta MS.

p. 111. A garden more fresh than the bower of Iram.[32]

5. Iram indeed is gone with all his rose.

I cannot ascertain whether FitzGerald had studied S. Rousseau's "Flowers of Persian Literature," which was published in 1801 as "a companion to Sir W. Jones's Persian Grammar," but at p. 71 of that work is an account of the "Garden of Iram," translated by Jonathan Scott from the تحفة المجالس (Tohfet al Mujālis). References to this fabulous garden, however, occur constantly in all Persian literature.

At pp. 123-124 occur quotations referring to the images of the Caravan in the desert, and the cock-crow rousing the apathetic sleepers. At p. 132, in an ode from Hāfiz we find

[30] از آمدن بهار از رفتن دي اوراق حيات ما ميكردد طي
[31] پرده داري ميكند در قصر قيصر هنكبوت بومي نوبت ميزند برگنبد افراسياب
[32] بوستاني تازه تر از گلستان ارم

the inaccessibility of the secrets of futurity and the ignorance of the wise on this subject,[33] and finally in the list of works recommended to the student at the end of the Grammar, we find the Salāmān and Absāl of Jāmī to which FitzGerald next turned his attention.

III. We have seen that, whilst FitzGerald's study of Jones's Persian Grammer was still in progress, he had obtained Eastwick's translation of the Gulistān of Sa'adi, but no record is preserved of the text which he used with it. It is readily comprehensible that a mind already strongly attracted by the Sufistic and antinomian verses of Hāfiz did not enter into warm sympathy with the rhapsodies of the essentially pious Sa'adi, but certain isolated passages must have impressed him, for we gather distinct echoes of them in his poem. The principal are as follows :

GULISTAN.[34]   FITZGERALD'S RUBA'IYAT.

CHAPTER I., Story 2.
    Many famous men have been
      buried underground
    Of whose existence on earth not
      a trace has remained,
    And that old corpse which had
      been surrendered to the earth
    Was so consumed by the soil
      that not a bone remained.[35]

Here again is a vivid picture of the transitory nature of earthly pomp, which is everywhere apparent in Omar Khayyām and in FitzGerald's poem.

    Story 9. I spent my precious life
      in hopes, alas !.
    That every desire of my heart
      will be fulfilled ;
    My wishes were realised, but to
      what profit ? since

[33] حديث از مطرب ومي گو وراز دهر کمتر جو که کس نکشود و نکشايد بحکمت اين معمّارا

34. I quote the Kama Shastra Society's translation, "Benares" (London, 1888), as being more literally accurate than the rhymed translation of Eastwick.

[35] بس نامور که زیر زمین دفن کرده اند کز هستیش بروي° زمین یك نشان نماند
و ان پیر اسفارا که سپردند زیر خاك   خاکش چنان بخورد کزو استخوان نماند

> There is no hope that my past life will return.
>
> * * *
>
> My life has elapsed in ignorance, I have done nothing—be on your guard![36]

This is quite in the spirit of Omar, and the quatrains in Fitz-Gerald's poem which echo the sentiment are too numerous to quote.

| Story 26. For how many years and long lives Will the people walk over my head on the ground?[37] | 23-4. Ourselves must we beneath the couch of earth Descend—ourselves to make a Couch—for whom? Ah! make the most of what we yet may spend, Before we too into the Dust descend.[38] |

In chapter ii. we find references to the hospitality of Hatim Tai (F. 10) and the sweet voice of David (F. 6). In chapter v. we recognise the "rumble of a distant drum" (F. 13), and in chapter vii. the image of the verdure and flowers sprouting from the clay of those who have died before us (F. 19-20). But these images are also to be found in Omar, so we can only say that FitzGerald met with them *originally* in the Gulistān.

IV. The Salāmān and Absāl of Jāmī occupies a small but not important place in this examination, for it was one of the works of which FitzGerald laboriously studied the original text and made a metrical paraphrase—his first printed volume. I have not read the original of this, save in a desultory and

[36] دريں اميد بسر شد دريغ عمر عزيز كه انچه در دلمست از درم فراز آيد
اميد بسته بر آمد ولي چه فايده زانكه اميد نيست كه عمر گذشته باز آيد

[37] چه سالهلي فراوان وعمرهاي دراز كه خلق برسر ما بر زمين بخواهد رفت

38. "FitzGerald had had before him a passage very analogous to this from the Bostān of Sa'adi, quoted in Sacy's notes to the Pend Nameh (*loc. cit.*, pp. 225-6), "After having brought and accumulated goods like the ant, hasten to consume them ere that thyself art consumed by the worms of the grave."

پس از بردن وگرد کردن چو مور بخور پیش از آن کت خورد کرم گور

superficial manner, for I found it difficult to arouse my own interest in it, but readers of FitzGerald's paraphrase will recognise many lines which contain thoughts which reappeared in his ruba'iyat. One passage, however, occurs in it to which especial reference must be made, and that is the couplet:

> Drinking, that cup of Happiness and Tears
> In which "Farewell" had never yet been flung.

It was from this that FitzGerald got the opening lines of his first edition:

> Awake! for Morning in the Bowl of Night
> Has flung the Stone that puts the Stars to Flight:

appending a note to the effect that the flinging of a stone into a cauldron was the signal for the breaking up of a company, such as a camp or halt of Arabs in the desert. The image occurs nowhere in Omar Khayyām.

V. The Mantik-ut-Tair of Ferīd-ud-dīn Attār is by far the most important of the materials under examination, for it is not too much to say that it might properly have been cited on the title-page of FitzGerald's poem as one of the sources of that work. It is one of the most important expositions that have come down to us of that alliance of religious revelation and mundane philosophy which the Muslims in general, and the Sufi philosophers in particular, have from all time attempted to demonstrate. The philosophical study of religions is neither more nor less than an attempt to solve the enigma of nature, and in Persia this study has been the constant care of the Sufis. They commence by the postulation of a vast Pantheism in which everything is God save alone God himself, everything being regarded by them as an emanation from God and everything being finally reabsorbed into God. As opposed to this, Muhammadanism is the gospel of the abstract and personal Unity of God, and it is interesting to note that Muhammad, admitting the personalities of Moses, the Prophets and Christ, looked upon Christianity as a kind of developed Judaism, which authorises us in concluding that Islam itself is nothing more than an aberration of Christianity.

Sufism, as it presents itself to the student of Omar Khayyām and Ferīd-ud-dīn Attār, has been admirably described by the great English traveller and Oriental scholar Sir Richard Burton; he says: "It is the religion of beauty, whose leading principle is that of earthly, the imperfect type of heavenly love. Its high priests are Anacreontic poets; its rites, wine, music and dancing, spiritually considered; and its places of worship, meadows and gardens where the perfume of the rose and the song of the nightingale, by charming the heart, are supposed to improve the mind of the listener."[39] The first Sufi (a word derived from صوف suf = wool, the material of which the robes of dervishes and fakirs are made) was one Abu Hashim Kufa, who lived in the second half of the eighth century A.D., so that Sufism was only two centuries old when Omar Khayyām flourished, and undoubtedly its greatest priest and poet was Muhammad bin Ibrahim Nishapuri Ferīd-ud-dīn Attār (meaning "Pearl of the Faith, the Druggist," from his trade, which was that of an oil-presser), born, as his name denotes, at Omar's own town of Nishapur in 1119 A.D., and massacred by the soldiers of Gengīz Khan in 1230, and in the 110th year of his age. The story of his conversion to philosophical religion is told to the effect that a Sufi Darvish apostrophized him one day in his shop, congratulating himself that he had no merchandise to carry on the Mystic Road, or Oriental "Way of Salvation," and exhorting Attār to prepare himself for the journey.

Attār, like almost every other Persian poet, wrote an immense quantity of verse, but his most interesting and important work is undoubtedly his "Language of Birds," a title which he borrowed from the passage in the Qur'ān, where Solomon declares, on his accession to the throne of David, "Oh, men! I understand the language of the birds."[40] No exposition of the doctrines of Sufism could be more complete than that

39. R. F. Burton. "Sindh, and the Races that inhabit the Valley of the Indus." London, 1851. Ch. viii., p. 201.
40. Chap. xxvii., v. 16.

contained in this book, and as those doctrines are prominent in the sentiments of Omar Khayyām, we may shortly state them, as follows:

> (i.) All created beings are emanations from God and are finally reabsorbed in God.
>
> (ii.) Since God orders all things, good and bad are indifferent, a doctrine identical with that of the early Christian schismatics called "Adamites," whose rites and tenets, by the way, leave much to be desired on the score of social ethics.
>
> (iii.) The soul is everything and the body imprisons it, therefore death is merely a return to God."[41]

And these doctrines are clothed in a wealth of imagery, often licentious, which, like the doctrine of Platonism, invoke God under the form of beauty, pleasure, and woman—which are one. It may be observed that the Sufis do not admit the contention of the strict Muhammadans that they are heretics; indeed, Attār himself, in the epilogue to this poem, says (as Omar said before him[42]), "I am neither a Muslim nor an infidel,"[43] and immediately after implores God to keep him firm in the faith of Islam,[44] and to make him die therein.[45]

I will now, following as far as possible the system observed above, point out some of the principal parallels between the Mantik-ut-Tair and FitzGerald's Ruba'iyat. The lines in the Mantik are counted by distichs (d).

41. Qur'ān, chap. i., v. 151: "We are of God and return to him."
42. "Beneath this heaven of azure marble I am neither an independent infidel nor a perfect Muslim," which is L. 527, C. 340, W. 347, N. 315, S.P. 314, P. 302, B. 532, B. II. 417.

ماييم دريں گنبد فيروزه رخام   نى كافر مطلق نه مسلمان تمام
43. d. 4592. I remain neither an infidel nor a Muslim,
   Between the two I remain bewildered.

من نه كافر نه مسلمان مانندهٔ   در ميان هر دو حيران مانندهٔ
44. d. 4595. Open this door to worthless me,
   And indicate a path to this pathless (lost) one.

بر من بيچاره ايں در بكشاى   ويں ز راه افتاده‌را راهى نماى
45 زيں همه آلودگی پاكم كنى   در مسلمانى فرو خاكم كنى

MANTIK-UT-TAIR.	FITZGERALD.
d. 4. To this (*i.e.*, the sky) he has imparted a perpetual motion.[46]	72. And that inverted Bowl they call the Sky, ... As impotently moves as you or I.
d. 24. The sky is like a bird that flutters along the path God has appointed for it.[47]	
d. 145. What is the sky, like a bowl turned upside down, unstable, stationary and revolving at the same time.[48]	
d. 2290. The sky is like a dish turned upside down.[49]	
d. 38. From the back of the Fish (Mahi) to the Moon (Mah) every atom attests Him.[50]	51. Taking all shapes from Mah to Mahi. They change and perish all, but He remains!

A score of passages might be quoted in which this figure occurs. FitzGerald's quatrain came, as a whole, from the Calcutta MS. (C. 72).

d. 147-8. Can he who during so many years... has impotently frequented the Door, know what is behind the veil.[51]	32. There was the Door to which I found no key; There was the Veil through which I might not see.

This is also an image which constantly recurs.

d. 152. Those who before us entered upon the Path have studied the Mystery time and again. They have agitated themselves profoundly and in the end their result is feebleness and astonishment.[52]	26. Why all the Saints and Sages who discuss'd Of the Two Worlds so wisely —they are thrust Like foolish Prophets forth; their words to scorn Are scattered and their Mouths are stopt with Dust.

[46] آن یکی را جنبش مادام داد

[47] مرغ گردون در رهش پر می زند   بر درش چون حلقه سر می زند

[48] چنبش کردون سر نگون ناپایدار   بی قراری دایما بر یك قرار

[49] هست کردون همچو طشتی سر نگون

[50] هر چه هست از پشت ماهی تا بماه جمله ذرات بر ذاتش گواه

[51] او چه داند تا درون پرده چیست
او که چندین سال برسر کشته است

[52] پیشوایانی که ره بین آمدند   گاه و بی گاه از پی این آمدند
جان خود را عین حسرت سوختند   همره جان عجز وحیرت سوختند

There is a quatrain in Omar (L. 326, C. 236, B. 322, W. 147, N. 120, S. P. 120) which is almost identical with this. At *d.* 216-8. Oh! Thou who pardonest my faults and acceptest my excuses, I am an hundred times consumed, why burn me again. It is by thy impulsion that my blood boils; let me shew my ardour.[53]

Here we have part of the sentiment of the quatuor of quatrains 78-81. There is a parallel quatrain for this in Omar, (L. 449, C. 286, W. 276, N. 236, S. P. 235, B. 445, B. ii. 308) but the whole of this great quatuor comes primarily from the parable quoted here; a little further on we find *dd.* 217 (*bis*[54]) to 220. "Oh! Thou my Creator! the good and the bad actions that I commit, I commit with my body. Pardon my weakness and efface my faults. I am led away by my natural instincts and cast by Thee into uncertainty; therefore the good and the bad I do comes from Thee."[55] And further, *d.* 225: "Thou hast planted in the centre of my soul a black mole (*i.e.*, original sin). Thou hast marked me with a spot as black as the skin of an Abyssinian; but if I do not become Thy mole, how can I become accepted by Thee? Therefore to attain that state I have made my heart like a black Abyssinian slave."[56] Here we have the original of the lines:

For all the Sin with which the face of Man
Is blackened, Man's forgiveness give—and take!

This plea for reciprocal forgiveness appears again with great force at *d.* 4618: "Deign to notice neither the good nor the bad that I have done. Since Thou createdst me gratuitously, Thou must pardon me gratuitously."[57] We shall presently

[53] اي كناه آموز عذر آموز من سوختم صد ره چه خواهي سوز من
خونم از تشوير تو آمد بجوش تا جوانمردي بسي كردم بهوش

54. By an error of the Editor the numbers 215 to 220 are repeated twice.

[55] خالقا گر نيك وگر بد كرده ام هر چه كردم با تن خود كرده ام
عفو كن دون همتيهاي مرا محو كن بي حرمتيهاي مرا

[56] هندوي جان بر ميان ارم ز تو داغ همچون حبشيا دارم ز تو
گر نيم هندوت چون مقبل شدم تا شدم هندوت رنگي دل شدم

[57] آفريدن رايكانم چون رواست بگذري از هر چه كردم خوب و زشت
رايكانم گر بيامرزي سزاست

find other passages in the Mantik-ut-Tair which contributed to this quatuor. We will proceed again with the parallel passages.

MANTIK-UT-TAIR.	FITZGERALD.
d. 240. So long as my Soul comes not forth to my lips, I will cherish these thoughts.[58]	43. And, offering his Cup, invite your Soul Forth to your Lips to quaff— you shall not shrink.
dd. 2501 and 3031 open passages containing this same metaphor.[59]	
d. 302. One night he (Muhammad) ascended to heaven, and all secrets were revealed to him . . . . . . from God he obtained complete understanding of all things.[60]	31. Up from Earth's Centre through the Seventh Gate I rose and on the Throne of Saturn sate; And many a Knot unravel'd by the Road.

The "Seven Gates," or "Seven Heavens," recur continually all through the poem, *sc. dd.* 271[61] and 1818,[62] etc. At *d.* 451 we find a reference to the life-giving breath of Jesus,[63] and at *d.* 453 to the White Hand of Moses.[64] At *d.* 742 *et passim* the loves of the Nightingale and the Rose.[65]

At *d.* 972. An observer of Spiritual Things approached the Ocean, and asked it why it was clad in blue (purple); why this robe of mourning . . . The Ocean replied . . . "I weep for my separation from The Friend.	33. Earth could not answer; nor the Seas that mourn In flowing Purple of their Lord forlorn.

[58] تا نیاید بر لبم این جان که بود   داشتم آخر دلی زان سان که بود
(a) در دم آخر که جان آمد بلب   کشف جانم بر لب آمد زانتظار
[59] (b) وقت مردن چو علی رودبار
[60] کرده در شب سوی معراجش روان   سرّ کل با او نهاده درمیان
هم زحق بهتر کتابی یافته°   هم کل کل بی حسابی یافته°
[61] در طلب برخود بکشف او هفت بار   هفت پرکار فلک شد آشکار
[62] خواست تا بشناسد اورا آن زمان   زو مکشف آگاه در هفت آسمان
[63] از دم عیسی کسی گر زنده خاست   او بدم دست بریده کرد راست
[64] در ضمیرش بود مکنونات غیب   زان بر آوردی ید بیضا زجیب
[65] طاقت سیمرغ نارد بلبلی   بلبلی را بس بود عشق گلی

> Since, by reason of my insufficiency, I am not worthy of him, I am clad in blue on account of the sorrow that I suffer."[66]

These are the two lines upon which Professor Cowell has given us the note which gave me the first clue for these researches. A curious illustration of FitzGerald's method is found in connection with the passage at *d.* 1017: "The true dawn was the light of his countenance."[67] This, together with Mr. Binning's note on the phenomena of the Oriental sunrise, produced his line and note concerning "the Phantom of False Morning." The process will be set out further on.

At *d.* 1559. We, all of us, leave the world like Wind, it has gone and we must go too.[68]	29. And out of it, as Wind along the Waste, I know not Whither, willy-nilly blowing.

This is one of two frequently recurrent images of death in Persian poetry; the other we find in *d.* 2288. "Knowest thou not that every man who is born, sinks into the earth and the wind disperses his elements,"[69]—a figure as frequently found in Omar as the former one.

At *d.* 1866. Heaven and Hell are reflections, the one of thy goodness, and the other of thy malice.[70]	68. Heav'n but the Vision of fulfill'd Desire, And Hell the Shadow from a Soul on fire.

Here, again, we have a true original, for there is no parallel for No. 68 in Omar. FitzGerald was reminded of it, but no

66 ديده ور مردي بدريا شد فرود
جامهٔ ماتم چرا پوشيدهٔ
داد دريا آن نكو دلرا جواب
چون زنا مردي نيم من مرد او
67 صبح صادق لمعهٔ از روي او
68 جمله چون بادي زعالم مي رويم
69 تو نميداني كه هر كو زاد مرد
70 طاعت روحانيان از بهر تست

كشت لي دريا چرا داري كبود
نيست هيچ آتش چرا جوشيدهٔ
كز فراق دوست دارم اضطراب
جامهٔ نيلي كرده ام از درد او
روح قدسي نفههٔ از بوي او
رفت او و ما همه هم مي رويم
شد بخاك و هر چه بودش باد برد
خلد و دوزخ عكس لطف و قهر تست

more, by quatrain 33 of the Bodleian, and 90 of the Calcutta MSS., which reads:

> The heavenly vault is the girdle of my weary body,
> Jihun is a watercourse worn by my filtered tears,
> Hell is a spark from my useless worries,
> Paradise is a moment of time when I am tranquil.[71]

We trace in this quatrain the original of "the Soul on Fire."

We find the first mention of "the rumble of the distant drum," at *d.* 2162, "He whose lofty station is indicated by the drum and the standard, cannot become a darvish,"[72] and at *d.* 2753, "Were it not better to strike the drum of sovereignty, etc.[73]

At *d.* 2340. He who controlled the world beneath his signet-ring (*i.e.*, Solomon) is actually an element beneath the earth.[74]

This figure occurs in various forms in Omar, and has been freely made use of by FitzGerald.

At *d.* 2342. The dead sleep beneath the earth, but though asleep they are anguished.[75]	29. . . . . the fire of Anguish in some Eye There hidden, far beneath and long ago.

Closely following these passages, we find the following fable:

d. 2345. (On a certain occasion) Jesus drank of the water of a clear stream whose flavour was more sweet than that of rose-water. By his side, a certain one filled his jar at this same stream and then withdrew. Then Jesus drank a little from this jar, and pursued his way, but now he found the water bitter, and stood amazed. "Oh, God!" he said, "the water of the stream and that in the jar are identical: explain to me the mystery of this difference in the flavour, why is the water in the jar bitter and that in the stream more sweet than honey." Then spake the jar these words to Jesus: "I am, of old, a man. I have been fashioned

[71] گردون کمری از تن فرسودهٔ ماست   جیهون اثری ز اشک پالودهٔ ماست
دوزخ شرری ز رنج بیهودهٔ ماست   فردوس دمی ز وقت آسودهٔ ماست

[72] هر که از کوس و علم درویش نیست   دور از و کان بانگ وبادی بیش نیست

[73] گفت تاکی کوس سلطانی زدن   زین نکوتر خشت نتوانی زدن

[74] آنکه عالم داشت در زیر نگین   این زمان شد توتیا زیر زمین

[75] جمله زیر زمین بر خفته اند   بلکه خفته این همه آشفته اند

a thousand times beneath the seven-domed heavens, now into a vase, now into a jar, and again into a bowl. They may refashion me again a thousand times, but I shall always be tainted with the bitterness of death. It so impregnates me that water contained in me can never be sweet."[76]

FitzGerald, in his paraphrase of the Mantik,[77] rendered this answer very beautifully:

> The Clay that I am made of, once was Man,
> Who dying, and resolved into the same
> Obliterated Earth from which he came
> Was for the Potter dug and chased in turn
> Through long vicissitude of Bowl and Urn:
> But, howsoever moulded, still the pain
> Of that first mortal Anguish would retain,
> And cast and re-cast, for a Thousand years
> Would turn the sweetest Water into Tears.

And it was from this passage of the Mantik, and from this alone, that we get the quatrain No. 38.

> And has not such a Story from of Old
> Down Man's successive generations roll'd,
> Of such a clod of saturated Earth
> Cast by the Maker into Human mould?

In the comment upon this parable in the Mantik we find the original of another quatrain of Fitzgerald that has no other source:

[76] خورد عيسي آبي از جوي خوش آب بود طعم آب خوشتر از گلاب
آن يكي زان آب خم هر كرد ورفت عيسي از خم نيز آبي خورد و رفت
شد زآب خم همي تلخش دهان باز كرديد و عجايب ماند ازان
گفت يا رب آب اين خم وآب جوي هر دو يك آبست سران بگوي
تا چرا تلخست آب خم چنين وان دگر شيرين‌ترست از انگبين
پس عيسي آن خم آمد در سخن گفت اي عيسي منم مرد كهن
زير اين نه كاسه من باري هزار كشته ام هم كوزه هم خم هم تغار
گر كنندم خم هزاران بار نيز نيست جز تلخي مركم كار نیز
دایم از تلخي مركم اين چنين آب من زانست نا شيرين چنين

77. This paraphrase was never published during FitzGerald's lifetime. It occupies pp. 433-452 of vol. ii. of his "Letters and Literary Remains." (*Vide* Note 12.)

d. 2355. Thou thyself art lost. Oh! Thou that pursuest the Mystery. Strive to discover it, ere thy life be reft from thee, for if, to-day, whilst thou livest thou findest not thyself, how then, when thou art dead, shalt thou unravel the secret of thine existence?[78]	53. But if in vain, down on the stubborn floor Of Earth, and up to Heav'n's unopening Door, You gaze *To-day* while You are You—how then *To-morrow*, You when shall be You no more?

The whole doctrine of the evanescence of the world is contained in the 27th chapter, which immediately follows this, and which contains the germ of one of FitzGerald's most sarcastic quatrains:

d. 2409. If thou seekest a moment of well-being in this world, Sleep! and then repeat what thou hast seen in thy dreams.[79]	65. The Revelations of Devout and Learn'd Who rose before us and as Prophets burn'd Are all but Stories which awoke from Sleep, They told their comrades and to Sleep returned.

It may be observed, however, that FitzGerald translated his quatrain from No. 127 of the Calcutta MS.

We come now to another most interesting side-light upon FitzGerald's mental process. There is in the Calcutta MS. (but not in the Bodleian MS. or Nicolas) a quatrain, No. 387, which may be thus rendered:

Neither thou nor I know the Secret of Eternity,
And neither can thou nor I read this Enigma.
There is talk of me and thee behind the curtain,
(But) When they raise the curtain there remains neither thee nor me.[80]

From this FitzGerald constructed two remarkable verses:

32. There was the Door to which I found no Key;
There was the Veil through which I might not see:

[78] خویش را کم کرده ای راز جوی پیش از آن کسی جان بر آید باز جوی
گر نیابی زنده خود را باز تو چون بمیری کی شناسی راز تو

[79] گر تو در عالم خوشی جوئی دمی خفته یا خواب میگوئی همی

[80] اسرار ازل را نه تو دانی و نه من وین حرف معما نه تو خوانی و نه من
هست از پس پرده گفتگوی من و تو چون پرده برافتد نه تو مانی و نه من

>   Some little talk awhile of Me and Thee
>   There was—and then no more of Thee and Me.
>
> 34. Then of the Thee in Me who works behind
>   The Veil, I lifted up my hands to find
>   A lamp amid the Darkness: and I heard,
>   As from Without, "*The Me within Thee blind!*"

There are those, I believe, "who by Genius and by Power of Brain" have found these two quatrains quite simple and self-explanatory. For my own part, I confess that I never understood them in the least until I found the two passages in Ferīd-ud-dīn Attār, which evidently surged up in FitzGerald's brain when he read the Calcutta quatrain. They are as follows:

d. 3090. The Creator of the world spoke thus to David from behind the Curtain of the Secret: "Everything in the world, good or bad, visible or invisible, is mere substitute, unless it be Me, Me for whom thou canst find neither substitute nor equal. Since nothing can be substituted for Me, do not cease to abide in Me. I am thy soul, be not separated from Me; I am necessary, thou art dependent upon Me . . . Seek not to exist apart from Me."[81]

and

d. 3735. "Since long ago, really, I am Thee and Thou art Me, we two are but one. Art thou Me or am I Thee, is there any duality in the matter? Or else, I am thee, or thou art me, or thou, thou art thyself. Since thou art me and I am thee for ever, our two bodies are one. That is all!"[82]

This is an admirable specimen of the Sufistic argument of Unity with God, or the Thee-in-Me that FitzGerald has introduced with such mystic skill into his Ruba'iyat.

[81] خالق الآفاق من فوق العجاب   كرد با داوود پيغمبر خطاب
كفت هر چيزي كه هست اندر جهان خوب و زشت و آشكارا و نهان
جملهرا يابي عوض الا مرا   نه عوض يابي و نه همتا مرا
چون عوض نبود مرا بي من مباش   من بسم جان تو تو جان كن مباش
نا گزير تو منم لي حلقه كير   يكنفس غافل مباش از نا گزير
لحظه‌ئي بي من بقائي جان مخواه   هر چه جز من پيشت آيد آن مخواه

[82] روزگاري شد كه تا شد بي شكي   من توئي و تو مني هر دو يكي
تو مني يا من توئي چند از دوئي   يا توم من يا تو من يا تو توئي
چون تو من باشي و من تو بردوام   هر دو تو باشيم يك تن و السلم

I have never found in Omar any mention of

> The Mighty Mahmoud Allah-breathing Lord
> That all the misbelieving and black Horde
> Of Fears and Sorrows that infest the Soul
> Scatters before him with his whirlwind Sword.

The reference is to Mahmoud the Ghasnawi, who made war upon the black infidels of Hindostān, whose conquest and its sequelæ are related at *d.* 3117 of the Mantik. The main image of the quatrain, the dispersal of fears and sorrows by wine, comes primarily to FitzGerald from a quatrain which is No. 81 in the Bodleian and No. 180 in the Calcutta MSS.

In like manner, though Omar is full of allusions to the dead that come not back again, the precise image of our ignorance of the road they travel comes from the Mantik:

d. 3205. No one has returned to the world after having travelled that Road, no one knows how many parasangs it extends ... Fool that thou art! how can those who have been lost in the Road for ever tell us of it.[83]	64. Strange is it not? that of the myriads who Before us pass'd the door of Darkness through Not one returns to tell us of the Road, Which to discover, we must travel too.

This passage is quoted in the Notes to De Sacy's Pend Nameh, where FitzGerald originally saw it.

At *d.* 3229 we find an allegory related by Amru Osman, in which we read of the presence of the Snake (Iblis) in Paradise at the moment of the creation of Adam (FitzGerald 81), and at *d.* 3248 Satan argues with the Creator quite in the manner of FitzGerald's great quatuor of quatrains: "If malediction comes from thee, there comes also mercy; the created thing is dependent upon thee since destiny is in thy hands. If maledic-

[83] وا نیامد در جهان زین راه کس نیست از فرسنگ او آگاه کس
چون نیامد باز کس زین راه دور چون دهندت آگهی ای نا صبور
چون شدند آنجایگه کم سر بسر کی خبر بازت دهند ای بیخبر